Around Cape Cod with Cap'n Goody in his Magic Whaleboat

Atlantic
Ocean

Provincetown

Cape Cod National Seashore

Plymouth

Truro

Wellfleet

Cape Cod Bay

"The
Mainland"

Eastham

Sagamore   Cape Cod Canal

Orleans

Sandy Neck

Brewster

Sandwich

Bourne

Dennis
Yarmouth

Chatham

Buzzards

Barnstable

Harwich

Bay

Otis
Air Force
Base

Mashpee

Hyannis

Hyannis
Port

Monomoy I.

Falmouth
Woods Hole

Nantucket Sound

Books by Paul Giambarba

Cape Cod Light

The Lighthouse at Dangerfield

Lighthouses

Whales, Whaling and Whalecraft

Surfmen and Lifesavers

Early Explorers of America

What Is It? at the Beach

Cape Cod Seashore Life

Around Cape Cod with Cap'n Goody

Going Whaling with Cap'n Goody

Blue Water Tales of old Cape Cod

Cape Cod Fact and Folklore

Around Cape Cod
with Cap'n Goody
in his Magic Whaleboat

written and illustrated by Paul Giambarba

36th Anniversary Edition

The Scrimshaw Press

P.O. Box 1795, Mashpee, Cape Cod, MA 02649
Discover more Cap'n Goody at www.scrimshawpress.com

To the real Lily and Andy
for whom this book was written,
and all my grandchildren.

Copyright © 2001 by Paul Giambarba

Library of Congress Card No. 65-27439

ISBN 0-87155-118-7

Printed and bound in the United States of America
Sixth printing, 2001

"Lily," Andy called out,
"I just found a clam!"

Lily looked up from her
book. An old gentleman nearby
looked up, too. He watched the
children and then he spoke in a
commanding voice, the kind of
voice you might hear booming
from the quarterdeck of a
mighty ship at sea.

"We don't call that a clam,
young man," he said loudly and
clearly. "We call it a KO-HOG.
That's spelled q-u-a-h-o-g."

"Quahog is what the Wampanoag Indians called it. Wam-pa-nog is how you say that."

"The Wampanoags were living and fishing here when the Pilgrims came ashore."

He waded toward the children. "Hold on a minute.
I'll show you how a quahog is different from other clams."
From his wire basket he took a quahog, opened it
with a knife and held it out for Lily and Andy to inspect.

"See, the shell is hard," he explained, "Inside there's
purple. The inside part is what the Wampanoags ground
into beads for wampum. Wampum is what they used as
money, like our dollars. Purple wampum was worth

twice as much as white wampum. Up in the city, people call the big quahogs Cherrystone Clams and the little ones Littleneck Clams."

The old man pointed to a hole in the wet sand. Andy stepped near it and water spurted out of the hole.

"Under there, on the other hand, is what *we* call a clam. Did you see him squirt when you walked by? I'll dig him up for you."

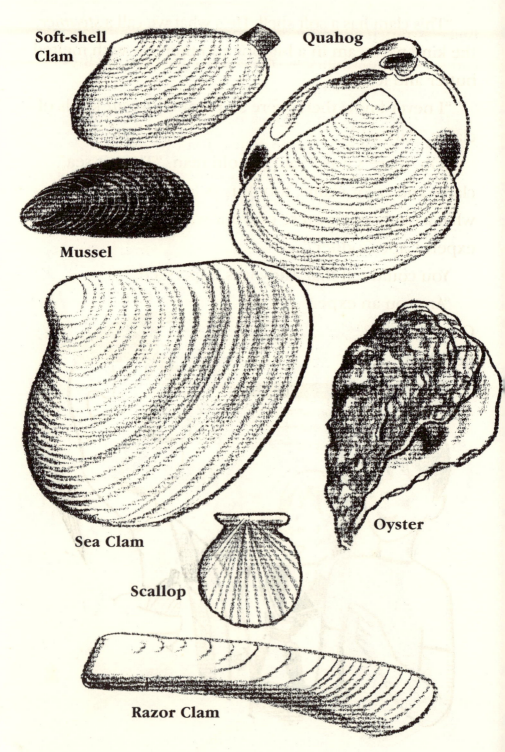

Soft-shell Clam

Quahog

Mussel

Sea Clam

Oyster

Scallop

Razor Clam

"This clam has a soft shell. He's what we call a *steamer*, the kind we steam in a big pot and then eat with melted butter and lemon."

"I never knew there were so many *different* kinds of clams," Lily said.

"Oh, there's lots," said the old man. "There's sea clams and razor clams, too. But as long as you know what a quahog is, you're on your way to becoming an expert Cape Codder."

You could tell that Andy was impressed.

"Are you an expert Cape Codder?" he asked.

"Am I an expert Cape Codder? Well, you might say that, young fellow. At least I'm an *old* Cape Codder," the old man said. "I'm Captain Goodman Nickerson Crosby Eldridge Hallett (and that's as many Cape Cod names as anyone can be called in a lifetime). But everybody knows me as Cap'n Goody, and you can call me that, too."

"Cap'n Goody?" repeated Lily.

"Cap'n Goody. I'm a hundred and sixty-seven years old and I've sailed the world around ten times or more. I know Singapore, the Indian Ocean, Tahiti, Moorea, Kamchatka, and the Bay of Naples like the back of my hand. I've lived through mutiny, typhoons, Confederate raiders and the grub on a whale ship three years out of Nantucket. My great-great-great-grandmother was a Wampanoag Indian princess. I guess you might say I'm an old Cape Codder all right."

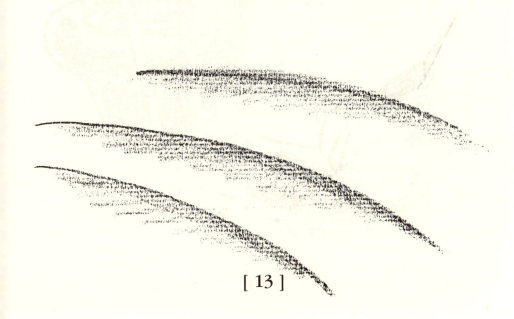

"Then you must know all about Cape Cod and everything, Cap'n Goody," Lily said.

"Well, I don't know all that much about everything. But I do know something about Cape Cod."

"If you young mainlanders want to come along with me, I'll give you the grand tour of a most unusual part of the United States of America."

"Oh, boy!" said Andy. "That sounds great!"

"Come along then," said Cap'n Goody. He led them to an open boat that was pulled up on shore. "The tide's coming in and we can cast off easily."

Within minutes they were all in Cap'n Goody's boat. They found what they supposed were life jackets under the seat. The Captain showed them how to put them on and how to stow them away, which is how he described storing them under the seats.

"Those jackets look a lot like parachutes," said Andy.

"They are," replied Cap'n Goody. "And when we shove off you'll see why we need them on board.

"Hang on! Here we go!"

In an instant they found themselves rising up, up, up – high into the sky!

"What kind of a boat is this, anyway?" asked Lily. Her eyes were wide with surprise.

"It's my magic whaleboat," announced the captain. "Don't be afraid. Just sit tight and don't rock the boat. I'm going to show you Cape Cod."

Cap'n Goody gestured with the long steering oar. "Down below there – that's Cape Cod Bay. The English explorer Bartholomew Gosnold anchored here. His crew caught so many codfish in the Bay that he called the place Cape Cod. All this land got pushed down by glaciers thousands of years ago and the shores are very dangerous. Surf breaks over sand bars away out from the beach. In a storm, ships can get blown into shore and break up in pieces on the bars. You can see the Cape Cod Canal down there and get an idea how it helps. Ships can cut through the canal now instead of going around the long and dangerous way."

Old Scusset Creek

Cape Cod Canal

Sagamore

Aptucxet Trading Post

Bourne

Old Manomet River

Buzzards Bay

Woods Hole→

Falmouth

Nobska Light

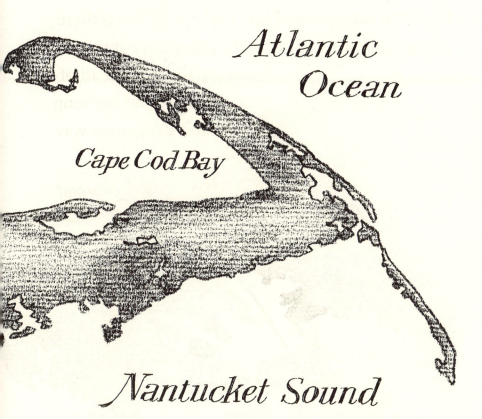

Atlantic Ocean

Cape Cod Bay

Nantucket Sound

"Let's go for a ride in the canal," suggested Cap'n Goody.

The next thing they knew they were in a steep dive, hanging on tightly to the sides of the magic whaleboat.

Fishermen lined both sides of the canal. Cars and trucks made their way across the Sagamore Bridge.

Behind the whaleboat loomed a large ocean freighter.

As they neared the Bourne end of the canal Cap'n Goody pointed out the railroad bridge that goes up like an elevator when ships pass underneath it. Just by the Bourne bridge he began sculling his oar – and the magic whaleboat left the water again.

As the boat hovered like a helicopter, Cap'n Goody pointed out the Aptucxet Trading Post.

"Three hundred years ago, the Pilgrim settlers established their first trading post here so that they could trade with the Dutch settlers of New York. Aptucxet is halfway across the Cape, in between two rivers."

"The Dutch would bring their goods along the Manomet River on the south and the Pilgrims would use Scusset Creek on the north. Part of the way to the Post was an overland haul for everybody – so the traders saw the need for a canal even then. Miles Standish, one of the Pilgrim leaders, had plans to build a canal right where it is now."

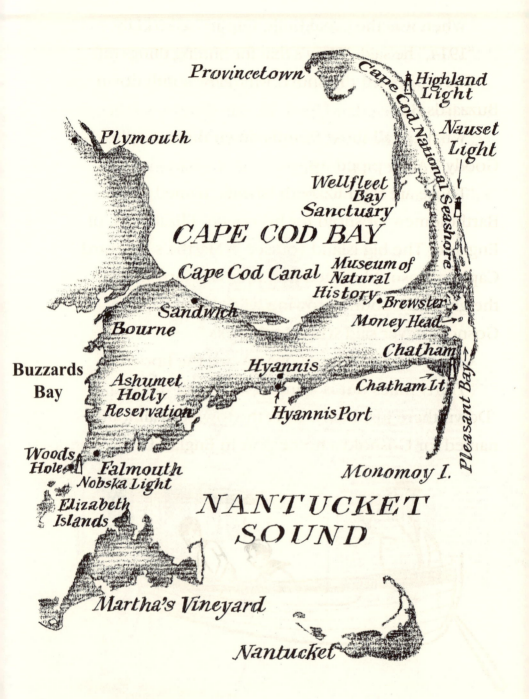

"When was the canal built, Cap'n?" asked Lily.

"1914," he said. "How's that for putting things off?"

They followed the shore, then flew south down Buzzards Bay.

"What are all those islands down there, Cap'n Goody?" Andy piped up.

"Those are the Elizabeth Islands, named by Bartholomew Gosnold for his queen, Elizabeth I, of England. The big island you see is Martha's Vineyard. Captain Gosnold named her, too. Vineyard was for the grapes he found growing wild there. Captain Gosnold never said who Martha was."

Cap'n Goody pointed out toward the horizon.

"Thirty miles out is Nantucket Island," he said. "Down there just below us is the town of Falmouth, named for Gosnold's home port in England."

"What is that place where all those boats are?" Lily asked.

"That's Woods Hole, where a lot of scientists are at work studying what goes on below the surface of the oceans. There's much more going on under the water than you might suppose. All through the sea move millions upon millions of living things. Well, at Woods Hole there are scientists who study these creatures from the deep.

"Some, from the Marine Biological Laboratory, study marine animals in special laboratories to find cures for diseases. Others, from the Woods Hole Oceanographic Institution, go out to sea in ships which are really

ATLANTIS II – a research vessel that sailed over a million miles, with 8,000 days at sea from 1963 to 1996.

ALVIN – a tiny submarine that made more than 3,500 dives and found a nuclear bomb accidentally dropped into the Mediterranean in 1966.

floating laboratories. They also use special vessels that dive like submarines to great depths."

"That sounds exciting!" Andy exclaimed.

" And not only do scientists study life in the sea," said Cap'n Goody, "they also make maps of the ocean floor. They use special equipment to find valleys, ridges and mountain ranges that form the ocean's floor. They have their own fleet of specially built vessels that can take scientists out for months at a time as far away as the Indian Ocean. They go all over the world to bring back valuable information."

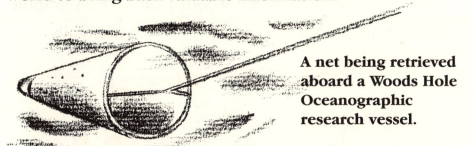

A net being retrieved aboard a Woods Hole Oceanographic research vessel.

The net collects samples of vegetable and animal plankton from the sea. This is plankton greatly magnified.

Cap'n Goody continued, "There's also an aquarium in Woods Hole that's run by the U.S. Fish and Wildlife Service. And over here on Nobska Point is Nobska Lighthouse."

"One of its windows is red!" said Andy.

'That's a sheet of red plastic. When the light flashes it casts a red glow on the water to let sailors know that there is some tricky going over the rocky shoals. All of Cape Cod's coast is dangerous to sailors. That's why there are so many lighthouses on the Cape."

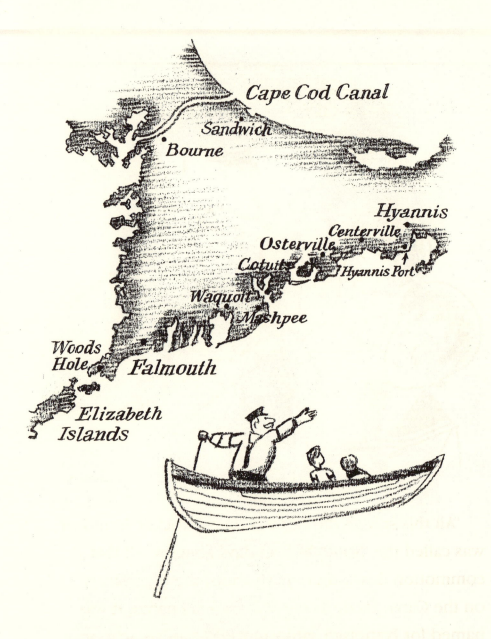

Cap'n Goody guided the magic whaleboat along the south shore from Falmouth to Hyannis.

"All this side of the Cape is on Nantucket Sound. It was called the 'South Sea' in days gone by. All that commotion down there is Hyannis, the biggest city on the Cape. Hyannis is a Wampanoag name. It was named for Iyanough, pronounced I-Yan-No, who was very kind and helpful to the first settlers. Hyannis used to be known as 'Iyanough's Land.' You can see how it got shortened to Hyannis."

"Is that Hyannis Port there, where President Kennedy used to live?" asked Andy.

"Yes, my boy, it is. And many's the time I used to see him with his family sailing out on the Sound in his sailboat, the *'Victura.'* A sloop she was, Wianno Senior class built over in Osterville, just back there a few miles."

"Mr. Kennedy was a fine young man, and he made a lot of us old Cape Codders proud. It was a great pleasure to know that the country and maybe a lot of the world was being run from Cape Cod. On summer weekends I'd see those helicopters coming over from Otis Air Force Base and I'd get a kick out of knowing that the President of the United States of America was up there in one of them and just itching to get home to the Cape."

So.Yarmouth

Dennis Port

Chatham

Hyannis

Harwich Port

W.Yarmouth

Great I.

Hyannis Port

Monomoy Island

From Hyannis Port the magic whaleboat continued eastward along the South Sea coast by West and South Yarmouth, Dennis Port, Harwich Port and Chatham.

"What's that long stretch of sand, Cap'n Goody?" asked Lily.

A French vessel of the type in which Champlain might have sailed.

"That's Monomoy – a dangerous stretch of sand bar and shoal water. It's feared by any who have come too close to shore in a roaring Nor'easter. Why, Champlain, the great French navigator, couldn't get to shore at Chatham until some Monomoy Indians rowed out to meet him and pilot his vessel in. That was way back in 1605. More than 200 years later the government put up a pair of lighthouses at Chatham. Everybody called them the 'Twin Sisters.' The ocean tore away the cliffs they were built on, so they were moved. One was moved over to Eastham, where it's now called Nauset Light."

Chatham's "Twin Sisters," about 1865.

"What did sailors do when their ship was wrecked?" Lily asked Cap'n Goody.

"They had to depend upon people who lived on shore. For a long time there were no lighthouses, nor any Coast Guard. It was up to brave Cape Cod men to row out through the crashing surf in their frail dories to save the crews on the sinking ships."

"They must have been very brave," Andy said.

"It took a lot of courage. Many times the dories would capsize in the violent seas and the rescuers themselves would drown. The U. S. Coast Guard has lost many men, too. It's a very dangerous business rescuing the crews of vessels in distress, especially in a howling Nor'easter or an ice storm."

**A Cape Cod lifesaving crew rowing to the aid
of a vessel in distress during a storm.**

Soon the magic whaleboat was headed up the Chatham coast past Orleans to Eastham. There Andy and Lily saw the bright red top band of Nauset Light.

"This area is all part of the National Seashore now," Cap'n Goody explained. "From here on up to Provincetown is all a national park."

"What are all those little cars on the beach, Cap'n?" asked Andy. "Are they what they call beach buggies?"

"They sure are. Do you want to go for a ride in one?"

"Do you mean it? Could we? Oh boy, you bet I would!"

In an instant they had beached the magic whaleboat and were all in a beach buggy.

"Hang on," warned the captain. "We're going to bounce around a bit."

Cap'n Goody explained the workings of a beach buggy.

"The tires are oversize and very smooth and wide.

"You've got to keep going so you don't get bogged down in the soft sand. Down by the water here where the

tide's gone out is the best place because the sand is pretty firm. But back up there in the dunes is very tricky driving even if you've got four-wheel drive."

Cap'n Goody stopped the beach buggy. Lily got out and ran to look for shells.

Andy found fishing tackle in the back of the buggy.
"Can we go fishing, Cap'n?" he asked.

"Sure. Come on. I'll show you two how to surf cast,"
said Cap'n Goody.

Lily said she couldn't imagine a fish that would bite a
hook on the end of a silly silver lure. Soon she found that
a bluefish would indeed bite a hook on the end of a silly
silver lure.

Cap'n Goody told her that a bluefish would bite a finger, too, if one got anywhere near his teeth.

Bluefish

Striped Bass

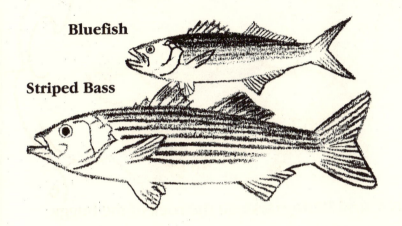

Within minutes Andy caught his first striped bass.

"This is more fun than clamming – er, quahogging!" he shouted.

Later on Cap'n Goody showed them how to clean a fish getting the messy job done while at the shore.

Then he told them about the great Outer Beach. It was called the "Back Side" in the old days and it's one of the most dangerous areas on the whole Atlantic coast.

"There are three lighthouses along this short stretch. You've seen the one at Chatham and this one here at Nauset. Well, there's a big one called Highland Light just a few miles up the beach at North Truro. That will give you an idea of just how bad this coast is."

"Have many ships been lost along here?" Andy asked.

"Hundreds and hundreds – fishermen, merchant ships, men o'war, even pirate ships!" said Cap'n Goody.

"PIRATES!" the children exclaimed. "Were there pirates on Cape Cod?!"

"I should say so," the captain answered. "There's a little island over in Pleasant Bay where the famous pirate, Captain Kidd, is supposed to have buried some

of his treasure. They call the isl[a
wouldn't be surprised."

The famous pirate, Captain Kidd
his treasure at a lonely beach.
Could it be Money Head?

Cap
that the
vessel v
pounce
King's §
seize th
was no
picked

The pir
captain
Sam Be
on the
quarter-
deck of
his pirat
galley
Whydah

"Wasn't
take thi

n Goody continued, "And it was on this very coast
pirate Sam Bellamy was wrecked in 1717. His
as cast up on the beach and the people of Orleans
d on it for the plundered treasure inside. The
overnment sent an officer down from Boston to
e wreck but by the time he got to Orleans there
hing left but the hull. The ship had already been
lean."

te

amy

hat against the law?" Lily asked. "I mean, to
gs like that – even from pirates?"

"Probably. But in those days most Cape folks were poor. Whatever floated in on the beach they considered theirs – and generally took it. That's how they got started whaling."

"You mean the whales swam up onto the beach?" Andy asked.

"Yes, boy. That's what's known as a drift whale. Some whales get caught on the sand bars that wreck ships. The tide goes out and leaves the whales helpless on the beach. This also used to happen to schools of blackfish, which are like small whales. Cape Codders would cut up these drift whales and boil down the blubber for oil. It's called 'trying' in great big 'try pots.' The oil was used as fuel for lamps. In those days there was no electricity.

A school of stranded blackfish

A *try pot* (about 250 gallons)

The try pots were bricked into the tryworks

Tryworks

"The Wampanoag Indians were the first whalers – and the settlers took right over. Soon they were out in small boats chasing whales and blackfish onto shore. It wasn't long before men put the try pots right on deck and went out to chase whales in mid-ocean."

Pieces of blubber were *tryed* to produce whale oil.

Oil was skimmed off by a *bailer*. When cool, it was packed into large barrels, which weighed 300 lbs. when full.

"Is a whale just a big fish?" asked Lily.

"No, it's not a fish," the captain answered. "It's a mammal, a warm blooded creature like you and me. And there are many, many kinds of whales. Right whales got their names because they were just the right kind to catch and 'try.' But it was the 'Sparm' whale that the old whalers really went after. The 'Sparm' whale has a 'case' of sperm oil in his head that is one of the purest oils anywhere. It brought a high price, and for that reason whalers chased that 'Sparm' whale to the four corners of the earth."

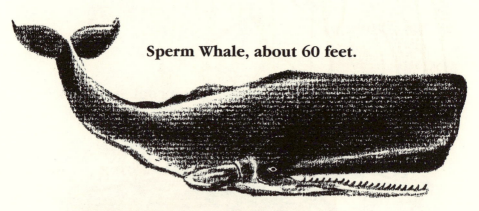

Sperm Whale, about 60 feet.

Right Whale, about 45 feet.

"Whaling ships would set out and wouldn't come home until every barrel they carried in the hold was full of whale oil. So, many whaling voyages lasted more than three years."

Whaling ships were broad of beam (which means very wide) and ungainly. They were built wide and stout in order to stow aboard as many barrels of oil as possible.

"The catching of the whale was done from whaleboats like the one we're in now. A whaleship carried three or four of these frail boats; each whaleboat carried five oarsmen and a boat steerer, who was also the harpooner. After striking the whale, he rushed to the stern of the boat to steer with the long steering oar."

Boat steerer and harpooner about to harpoon a whale.

*A **Nantucket Sleighride.***

"The harpoon was attached to a long line of over 1,000 feet. Usually the wounded whale sounded (dove below the water) but if it swam away furiously it took a whaleboat on what was called a 'Nantucket Sleighride.'"

After they climbed back in the magic whaleboat, Cap'n Goody took Lily and Andy high above the long arm of land that stretches from Eastham to Provincetown.

"Down there you'll see one of the best things to happen to Cape Cod since the days of sails and whales," he pointed out. "From here to Provincetown, most of the Cape is part of the Cape Cod National Seashore."

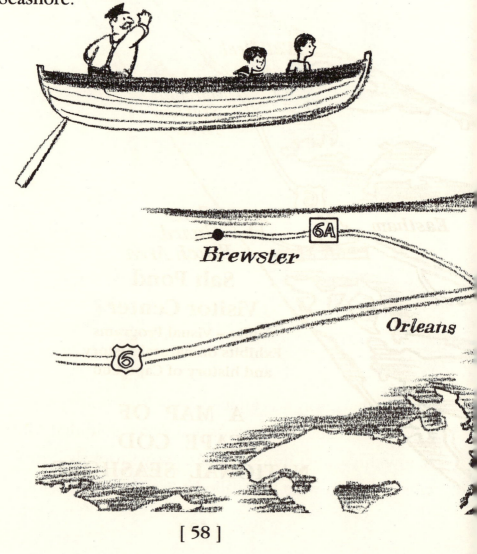

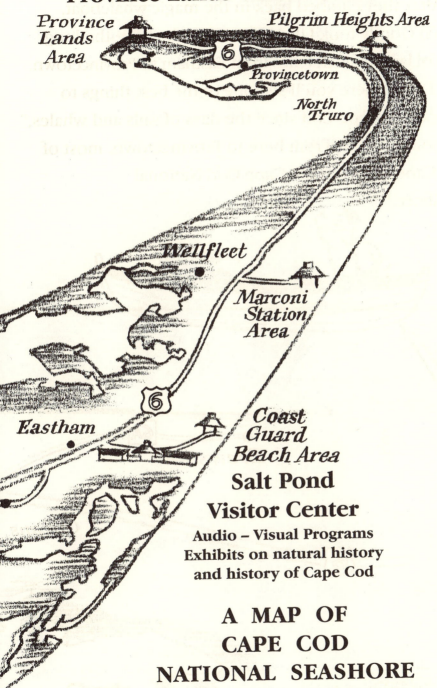

Province Lands Visitor Center

Province Lands Area

Pilgrim Heights Area

6

Provincetown

North Truro

Wellfleet

Marconi Station Area

6

Eastham

Coast Guard Beach Area

Salt Pond

Visitor Center

Audio – Visual Programs
Exhibits on natural history
and history of Cape Cod

A MAP OF
CAPE COD
NATIONAL SEASHORE

"What's a National Seashore?" Andy asked.

"A National Seashore is a government park – just like Grand Canyon or Yellowstone and those big areas out West. Government parks are run by the National Park Service and belong to all the people of the United States. This seashore park has thousands of acres, and it will be kept just the way you see it now – miles and miles of beaches and marshes. That's the way the Pilrgrims saw it."

Cape Cod, as it probably looked 350 years ago.
The tall timber was cut down long ago by the early settlers.
A rough dwelling of the period stands in the clearing.

"You see, said Cap'n Goody, "people change things. More and more people are coming to Cape Cod all the time – you've seen all the houses being built. Well, to build houses you need land to build them on. And to get that land, you have to clear out woodlots. When you take woodland, you chase out birds and wildlife, and cut off the food supply for shellfish, small worms, and things fish eat."

Tidemarshes support shellfish eaten by humans.

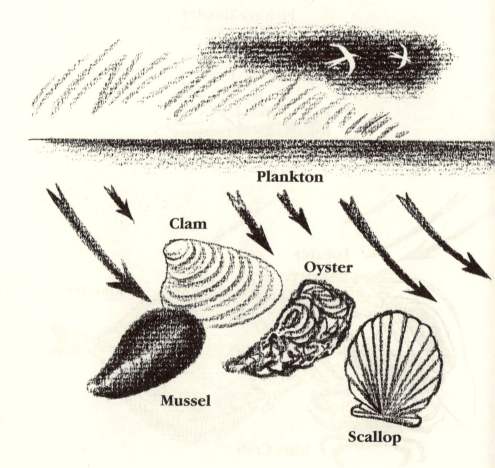

Plankton

Clam

Oyster

Mussel

Scallop

"The fish go, the birds and other wildlife die or go somewhere else. Houses go up. One town runs into the next town and before you know it, it looks like everyplace else. In 1961, the Department of the Interior made this part of the Cape Cod seashore a National Park so that it will keep its special kind of beauty."

Plankton from tidemarshes feeds creatures eaten by humans.

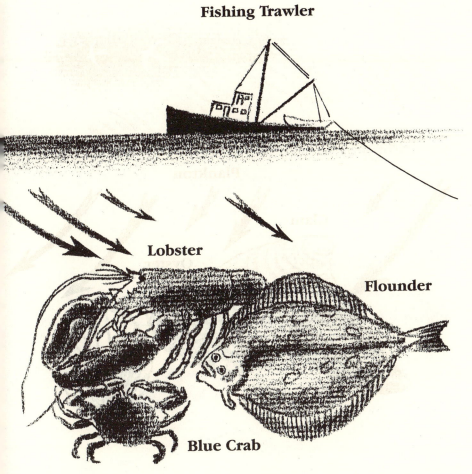

Fishing Trawler

Lobster

Flounder

Blue Crab

Flying over Wellfeet in the magic whaleboat, the
children were startled by loud honking, as if people in
hundreds of automobiles were sounding their horns.

"What's that?" cried Lily, as a flight of geese noisily
passed by.

"Those are Canada Geese," said Cap'n Goody.
"We're right over the Wellfleet Bay Wildlife Sanctuary of
the Massachusetts Audubon Society. It's one of the
most spectacular shorebird areas in this part of the
country."

"What's a shorebird?"

"Shorebirds are birds which live and feed on the
seashore – like gulls and terns, sandpipers and plovers.
Look here, I'll point
out some for you. . . ."

Ruddy Turnstone

Common Tern

Herring Gull

[65]

Canada Goose

Black Duck

Pectoral Sandpiper

Willet

Greater Yellowlegs

Knot

Piping Plover

Semipalmated Plover

Sanderling

Semipalmated Sandpiper

"Cape Cod sure is full of nature, isn't it?" Andy
exclaimed.

"Cape Cod is full of history," Cap'n Goody
answered. "The history of people, and natural history,
too – the history of animals and plants."

"We have that in school," Lily added.

"Well, you can learn that down below, too, at the
Wellfleet Bay Sanctuary."

"Can you learn about flowers and trees down
there?" Lily wanted to know.

"Certainly. In fact, we'll get a head start right now.
Let's find some." Cap'n Goody nosed the whaleboat
down to a gentle landing. The children got out and
followed him along a marked trail. Cap'n Goody
pointed out some plants found on Cape Cod.

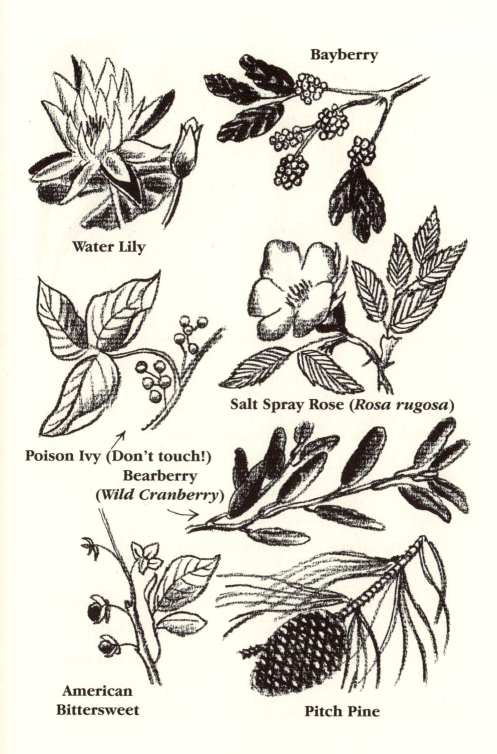

Bayberry

Water Lily

Poison Ivy (Don't touch!)

Salt Spray Rose (*Rosa rugosa*)

Bearberry
(*Wild Cranberry*)

American
Bittersweet

Pitch Pine

"I'm a little bit tired, Cap'n Goody," Lily said. Her head was humming with all she and Andy had seen and done in just one afternoon of vacation. "There's so much to do here."

"Oh, but this is only part of it," Cap'n Goody said.

"You haven't seen anything by any means. We've just scratched the surface! You haven't seen the Cape Cod Museum of Natural History in Brewster. You can learn a lot there about wildlife, trees and flowers, insects and such. During Spring and Autumn, school children from all over Cape Cod go there in school buses."

Cap'n Goody could see that the children's eyes looked sleepy.

Once back in the magic whaleboat, the children yawned and yawned. Cap'n Goody headed the whaleboat in the direction of home and slipped silently through the late afternoon breeze. The gentle motion put Andy and Lily to sleep.

The next thing they heard was Cap'n Goody calling out, "WAKE UP, WAKE UP, we're home."

The magic whaleboat touched down on the beach where Andy had dug up a clam – er, quahog – and the children climbed out.

Lily looked around to thank Cap'n Goody, but all she saw was Andy doing the exact same thing. Both had their mouths open for the start of a sentence that began, "We had a wonderful time – "

But Cap'n Goody was gone. The magic whaleboat was also gone, vanished without a trace!

And that is the story of Cap'n Goody and his magic whaleboat, at least for now. To Lily and Andy the Cape now looks like more than just another beach or vacation place. They often return to the same spot where Andy dug up quahogs in the hope of meeting the good captain again.

Perhaps, one day. . . .

THE AUTHOR acknowledges the help, encouragement and assistance given him in the beginning by so many generous souls and lovers of books for children, foremost among them Marion Smith, of Lorania's Books and Toys, Hyannis; Pat Patterson, of Bayberry Books and Toys, Orleans; Naturalist Bob Taylor, of Cape Cod National Seashore; Ruth Hill Viguers, Editor of *Horn Book* magazine; Fridolf Johnson, Executive Editor of *American Artist* magazine; Alden Johnson, President of *Barre Publishers*; and Dana Marston, *Major, USMC, retired,* who was – as Cap'n Marston of Osterville – the inspiration for Cap'n Goody.

About the Author

Paul Giambarba began *The Scrimshaw Press* over 30 years ago to make available abundantly illustrated original material in quality paperbacks at modest prices. His mission: to write and illustrate books that interest young readers in the world around them, and the local environment of Cape Cod that is so full of history and the wonder of nature.

Giambarba received his training as an illustrator from Harold Irving Smith, a pupil of the great painter and teacher Robert Henri (1865-1929). In his 35 years as a graphic designer for Polaroid Corporation, Tonka Toys, and others, he won many awards and international recognition for his work. He is the author and illustrator of 18 titles published by *The Scrimshaw Press; Atlantic/ Little, Brown; Houghton-Mifflin, Doubleday,* and others. He has been a resident of Cape Cod since 1960.

Edward Rowe Snow, dean of New England marine historians, described the author as: ". . . the young person's best friend," and wrote " . . .this genius of the Cape has produced . . . books which children will enjoy and from which readers of any age can profit."